Why do we say that?

Why do we say that?

Compiled by
Graham Donaldson
and
Sue Setterfield

DAVID & CHARLES
Newton Abbot   London   North Pomfret (Vt)

*A number of the sayings in this book have
previously appeared in the* Daily Mail

British Library Cataloguing in Publication Data

Donaldson, Graham
  Why do we say that?
    1. Aphorisms and apothegms
    I. Title II. Setterfield, Sue
    398'.9'21   PN6271

    ISBN 0–7153–8938–6

Photoset in Syntax
by Northern Phototypesetting Co, Bolton
and printed in Great Britain
by Billings Limited, Worcester
for David & Charles Publishers plc
Brunel House Newton Abbot Devon

Published in the United States of America
by David & Charles Inc
North Pomfret Vermont 05053 USA

Introduction

When we use expressions like 'He's leading the life of Reilly' or 'That's a load of old codswallop' we take it for granted that people automatically know what we mean – usually, they do.

But how many people know the origins of these everyday sayings, many of which go back centuries?

In some cases the roots are irretrievably lost in the mists of antiquity. In other cases, more than one theory exists for an expression's origin. And in still other cases, confusion has arisen when an existing saying has been adopted to fit a new circumstance.

For example, the saying 'Nine-day wonder' which originally referred to the time-span normally taken by new-born kittens or puppies to open their eyes, subsequently neatly fitted the unfortunate fate of Lady Jane Grey who reigned as Queen of England for nine days in July, 1553, before being executed the following year. Her plight is often – we believe incorrectly – put forward as the basis of the 'Nine-day wonder' expression.

The origins of many everyday sayings listed in this book *are* beyond dispute. Where differing theories do exist we have selected the one we consider to be the most likely.

The delights and surprises contained in these pages will undoubtedly leave you feeling 'over the moon'. Talking of which . . .

Buying a pig in a poke

At some time or other we've all been warned not to buy a 'pig in a poke'! But how did that saying originally come about?

To buy a pig in a poke means that you have been cheated. Back in Saxon times a suckling pig would be taken to market and sold in a sack, or poke. However, there were some shady characters around, and an unsuspecting buyer could find that a cat had been substituted for a pig in the poke.

To go on strike

This has its roots in the eighteenth century when life at sea was lonely and cruel, with harsh punishments handed out to offenders. But seamen sometimes got together to fight their bad conditions. They would strike the sails of their ships – which means to lower them – so preventing the ship leaving port until their grievance was settled.

A feather in your cap

If your boss said this to you it would mean that you had done something praiseworthy and had gone up in his estimation. It goes back to the days when the Red Indians were on the warpath. For every enemy a brave killed he was allowed to add a feather to his head-dress.

Put a sock in it!

In these days of compact discs, videos and digital recordings, it is astonishing to think that only fifty years ago people used wind-up gramophones with the sound emerging from a large horn. A volume control was a thing of the future. So, when Aunt Agatha complained of that dreadful Charleston noise there was only one thing to do – put a sock in it – literally.

One or more woollen socks were pushed into the horn of the gramophone to muffle the sound. Today it means, quite simply; 'shut up'.

Crocodile tears

To weep crocodile tears means to fake sadness. If you were to look closely (but not too closely!) at a crocodile while he was eating a large meal you would see tears in his eyes. You could be excused for thinking he was a bit upset for his victim. Not a bit of it.

In fact the crocodile has a duct at the corner of each eye which automatically releases 'tears' when he opens his jaws wide. He may look sorry for his victim but don't you believe it. He's just shedding 'crocodile tears'.

Sent to Coventry

If you are sent to Coventry it means that people around you deliberately ignore you and will not speak to you because you have done something to upset them.

During the English Civil War there was such huge support in Coventry for the Parliamentarians that any Royalist prisoners from neighbouring Midland towns were sent there because it was certain they would receive no help. Indeed, the great majority of Coventry Parliamentarians not only refused to speak to the Royalists, but acted as though they didn't exist.

The boot's on the other foot

Today, this expression is used when a situation is quite the reverse of what it was originally. It was only 200 years ago that footwear makers began manufacturing left and right shoes and boots. Before that, they were the same for both feet.

A man who tried on his new boots often found that if one of them hurt, his problem could be solved by swapping them over. A total change had come about – the boot was on the other foot.

What a white elephant

A white elephant is a grand plan or scheme, usually fantastically expensive, but which, in real terms, is quite useless. Hundreds of years ago white elephants were regarded as sacred. To harm or neglect them was an offence punishable by death.

The King of Siam sometimes gave a white elephant to an enemy as a gift – knowing full well that he would probably be ruined, having to spend a fortune looking after it.

A pretty kettle of fish

When somebody lands in a tricky, difficult, or awkward situation, they might well say, 'this is a pretty kettle of fish'.

Years ago it was the custom in the Border regions of Scotland to go on riverside picnics where salmon would be caught, boiled on the riverside in a kettle – a cooking pan – and eaten on the spot. Such picnics became known as a 'kettle of fish'.

The word 'pretty' originally meant 'tricky'. So, when the picnickers were having trouble landing their salmon, which apparently happened a lot, they would be faced with a pretty kettle of fish.

Barking up the wrong tree

If you complain or protest about something without good reason, or put the blame for something on the wrong person, you are barking up the wrong tree.

The saying comes from the practice of raccoon-hunting in America which has to be done at night when the small, furry animals are about. Dogs chase the raccoons and guide hunters to where they have seen them try to hide in branches. But sometimes, in the dark, the dogs make a mistake and 'bark up the wrong tree'.

Back to square one

This means that a plan has been abandoned and you are starting again from the beginning. It comes from the early days of radio commentaries on football matches before the likes of Brian Moore or John Motson.

To make it easier for the listener to follow the game, a diagram of the pitch was published, divided into squares and the commentator would continually refer to which square the ball was in.

The goalkeeper was in square one and if the ball was returned to him by a defender to start a fresh attack, it was 'back to square one'.

Cash on the nail

This saying means that you must pay cash immediately for your purchases. In this case, credit cards will not do nicely thank you.

It developed in the market places of England hundreds of years ago when a pole, or nail, was erected by traders.

They were the forerunners of shop counters – the buyer put his money on the nail and the seller put any change on the nail too, so everyone could see their dealing was done openly and fairly.

Climb on the bandwagon

This saying is used to describe anybody who joins in with something that looks like it will be a success, so that they can make a profit for themselves.

It comes from the days when a band used to play on a wagon driven through the streets of towns in the southern States of America to advertise religious or political meetings.

When there was an election, important people would climb on the bandwagon to demonstrate their support for a candidate.

Swinging the lead

A person who pretends to be working when he is doing nothing, or claims to be ill when there is nothing wrong with him, is said to be 'swinging the lead'.

Before today's sophisticated navigational equipment, seamen used to find out the depth of water by dropping a lead weight, attached to a thin, marked rope, to the bottom of a waterway.

Some lazy sailors, would take as long as possible about it. They would swing the lead to and fro several times instead of just dropping it straight into the water.

To strike while the iron is hot

If you act at exactly the right time, then you strike while the iron is hot and things work out just right. It is a saying that goes back hundreds of years and refers, not surprisingly, to the skills of the village blacksmith.

His experience and knowledge enabled him to know just when to start hammering on a horseshoe to form the right shape. It would work only when the metal was just at the right temperature. He had to strike while the iron was hot.

On your beam ends

When you are absolutely out of luck, out of money and out of much else besides, you are said to be 'on your beam ends'.

It's a phrase borrowed from old nautical times. A wooden ship depended for stability on its beams — the timbers that ran across the vessel, holding the sides in place and supporting the deck. A ship that was wrecked or so badly damaged that it was lying on its side, was 'on its beam ends'.

Eating humble pie

To eat humble pie means to be humiliated, to admit others know best or are superior in some way.

The saying comes from the days when the Lord of the Manor and his fellow huntsmen feasted on the spoils of their day's hunting. They ate prime venison, while the servants and others of low standing had to make do with a pie made from the umbles of the deer – its entrails, liver and heart.

Working to a deadline

A deadline is the final time by which a job must be finished. Journalists use the word a lot. If they don't meet their deadline their work is useless – or 'dead' – because it will have missed the edition.

The phrase comes from the American Civil War in the 1860s. A line was marked all round the wire fence of the Andersonville prisoner-of-war camp and any prisoner seen crossing the line was, without warning, shot dead.

Bring home the bacon

To 'bring home the bacon' is to return home triumphantly, having achieved some plan or objective, perhaps a pay rise or promotion at work.

The saying refers to the custom of the Dunmow Flitch which dates back nearly 900 years. Any person kneeling at the church door in the village of Dunmow, Essex, who swore that for a year and a day he had never had an argument with his wife or wished himself unmarried, could claim an award. It was a flitch (or side) of bacon. But only eight people won it in more than 500 years.

Apple of your eye

If someone referred to you as the apple of their eye it would mean that they are particularly fond of you – usually when you've done something to make them proud!

It was long believed that the pupil of the eye was a round, solid ball – rather like an apple. For that reason the pupil was called the eye's apple.

Sight, of course, has always been held as one of man's most precious assets. So anybody deeply cherished by another person became as important to him as 'the apple of his eye'.

I could sleep on a clothes line

When people are really exhausted and tired out, they sometimes say 'I could sleep on a clothes line'.

They are lucky they don't have to. In the last century in big cities like London, poor people had to do just that.

Landlords of inns used to charge people twopence a night to sleep sitting up on a bench, leaning against a line stretched tight in front of them. It was known as the 'twopenny rope'. Often, callous landlords would wake their guests in the morning simply by cutting the rope.

Caught eavesdropping

There are a lot of stories in the news today about 'phone-tapping' and 'bugging'. People who do it are the high-technology counterparts of the centuries-old 'eavesdropper' – somebody who listens in to other people's private conversations.

The eaves of a house are the parts of the roof that stick out over the walls, protecting them from falling water. The space on the ground where the water falls was known originally as the 'eavesdrip' and later as the 'eavesdrop'. This was the area where people like blackmailers, or even detectives, would hide, hoping to hear what was going on in the house. Such people became known as 'eavesdroppers'.

A nine-day wonder

Something that is very popular for a while and then loses its appeal is said to be 'a nine-day wonder'.

The saying is said to come from the plight of newborn puppies and kittens which are, of course, blind at birth. Generally, their eyes open about the ninth day of their lives.

So for the first nine days all is wondrous and mysterious. After that they can see things clearly and the world around them becomes commonplace and taken for granted. The 'nine-day wonder' is past.

To put a spoke in your wheel

If you are trying to get on with something and somebody does something to stop you, they have 'put a spoke in your wheel'.

In olden days the wheels on carts were solid, but they had one or two holes in which the driver could place a pin. This pin, or spoke as it was called, was used either in the same way as a parking brake on the modern car, or to prevent the cart running out of control, as a horse could not go far if it had to drag the spoked wheels.

Nineteen to the dozen

This saying is used of somebody who talks very quickly. Patrick Moore, who presents the TV programme, The Sky at Night, is often said to be talking 'nineteen to the dozen'.

The expression came about in the tin and copper mines of Cornwall which were often hit by disastrous floods. But in the eighteenth-century, steam-powered pumping engines were invented to clear the water. At the peak of their efficiency the pumps were said to be working at 'nineteen to the dozen', meaning that they were pumping out 19,000 gallons of water for every twelve bushels of coal needed to keep the engines going.

A flash in the pan

A 'flash in the pan' describes somebody who shows great promise, then fails to live up to expectations.

For example, a darts player might score the maximum 180 with his first three darts. Onlookers think he is a potential champion. But he is unable to repeat it. His earlier success was a mere 'flash in the pan'.

The expression came from the early seventeenth-century flintlock – a very unreliable musket. When its owner pulled the trigger there would often be a dramatic flash in the lock-pan. But the powder failed to ignite so the gun would not fire.

Having an axe to grind

This saying describes a person who tries to persuade somebody else to adopt a course of action without revealing their own selfish interest.

The saying comes from a story told by American inventor Benjamin Franklin. When he was young, a man brought an axe into the yard where Franklin was working and asked the boy to show him how the grindstone worked. When, after much hard work, the axe was ground, the man laughed at Franklin and left, carrying his newly sharpened axe.

Tell it to the Marines

People who relate stories that nobody believes are often told 'go tell it to the Marines!'

Just over 300 years ago Charles II didn't believe a word when a traveller told him he had seen flying fish. But when a Marine vouched for the story, the King decreed it must be true. He said, 'No class of our subjects can have so wide a knowledge of seas and lands as the men of our loyal Maritime Regiment of Foot'.

Henceforward, ere ever we cast doubts about a tale that lacks likelihood, we will first 'tell it to the Marines'.

Possession is nine points of the law

Somebody who uses this saying is claiming to have an overwhelming advantage over his opponent in a quarrel. He is saying that his case is so strong it would be very difficult for the other person to win.

The original nine points of the law were; 1 A lot of money; 2 A lot of patience; 3 A good cause; 4 A good lawyer; 5 A good counsel; 6 Good witnesses; 7 A good jury; 8 A good judge; 9 Good luck!

Sold down the river

If somebody betrays you or breaks a promise, then they are said to have 'sold you down the river'.

The phrase arose in the United States in the last century when rich American householders would sell their slaves to plantation owners. The slaves would have to leave the relative comforts of the big houses and be transported down the Mississippi river to a harsh and cruel life on the plantation.

Bury the hatchet

People who have been locked in an argument for some time might well decide at some stage to 'bury the hatchet'. In other words, they will end their feud and forget their differences.

When one of the North American Indian tribes wanted to end a war, either against another tribe or against the white man, the first thing was to smoke the peace-pipe. Then they would be 'commanded by the Great Spirit' to bury their hatchets, knives and other weapons as a positive sign of their wish for peace.

Chancing your arm

Somebody who takes a risk to gain an advantage for himself is 'chancing his arm'.

It was originally a military saying and referred to the fact that insignia of rank, like badges or stripes, were worn on the arm of a soldier's uniform. If he broke the King's Regulations in any way, he was 'chancing (that is, risking) his arm'.

Lock, stock and barrel

If somebody emigrated to Australia they might decide to sell their house and contents — 'lock, stock and barrel'. In other words, everything they possess. The phrase means something in its entirety.

Its origins, however, have nothing to do with door locks, shop stocks or barrels of beer. It is simply an old military reference to mean everything, the whole lot . . . the lock, stock and barrel of a firearm is the complete gun.

Feeling badgered

If you tease or annoy somebody and will not leave them alone, you are said to be badgering them.

The saying comes from the cruel medieval sport of badger-baiting. The poor animal was put into a large, upturned barrel, then dogs were sent in to drag him out. When they emerged, the badger was separated from the tormenting hounds and sent back in the barrel to recover – only for the dogs to be unleashed upon him over and over again.

At sixes and sevens

A person is said to be 'all at sixes and sevens' when he is faced with a difficult problem and just doesn't know what to do.

The phrase comes from a dispute in the middle ages between two of the craftsmen's guilds in the City of London. The Merchant Taylors and the Skinners were both founded within a few days of each other in 1327, five other guilds having already been chartered. For nearly fifty years they argued about which was to go sixth and seventh in processions. Finally, in 1484, the Lord Mayor ruled that they should take it in turns — whoever was sixth one year, would be seventh the next . . . and so on.

A baker's dozen . . .

This phrase means, quite simply, thirteen, not twelve. It comes from olden days when bread was the staple diet of the population and there were heavy penalties for any baker whose loaves were of short weight.

So to make sure they didn't fall foul of the law, many bakers used to add an extra loaf – called the vantage loaf – to each batch of twelve.

The Best Man

He, of course, is the chap who remembers the ring, reads the telegrams, and generally helps the bridegroom at a wedding.

According to Scottish legend, however, his duties used to be much more demanding. For it was customary for a man in love simply to kidnap and unceremoniously carry off the woman he had fallen for. He would choose good friends to help him in the task – groomsmen – and the bravest became known as the 'Best Man'.

The bride's closest friends – bridesmaids – were supposed to help her defend herself against her abductors. No doubt they both lived happily ever after!

Not enough room to swing a cat

When an estate agent describes a house as 'compact' what he probably really means is that it is tiny – that there is 'not enough room to swing a cat'.

The 'cat' in this centuries-old saying is not a furry puss but the dreaded nine-thonged whip, known as the 'cat o' nine tails' that was used to punish sailors. The punishment always took place on deck because below there was 'not enough room to swing a cat'.

A whipping boy

A person who is punished or blamed for an offence that somebody else has committed is often known as 'a whipping boy'.

In the middle ages it was common practice in European countries for a boy of common birth to be educated alongside a royal prince. But he paid heavily for the privilege. If the prince did something wrong, discipline demanded that punishment be inflicted. But there was no question of the royal bottom being spanked; the commoner had to step (or rather, bend) forward and he was flogged instead. Such was life for a 'whipping boy'.

Conspiracy of silence

If you are the victim of a 'conspiracy of silence' you are convinced –
often wrongly – that your friends or associates are trying to keep a
secret from you.

The expression was first used in Victorian times by a poet named
Sir Lewis Morris. In truth he was not very good, but he wanted to
become Poet Laureate. He complained to writer Oscar Wilde, that
people were jealous of him and so refused to discuss his poetry.
'There is a conspiracy of silence against me. What shall I do?' he
asked. Oscar replied 'Join it'.

Get your goat

If somebody 'gets your goat', they annoy, irritate, or generally make you angry. And if, years ago, you were a racehourse owner, you would have had good reason to be upset for it was a trick of the trade to stable a thoroughbred racehorse with a goat, the belief being that the presence of the smaller animal kept the horse calm and composed. Knowing this, it was not uncommon for some rascals to break in, separate the two animals, thus upsetting the highly-strung horse and probably causing it to lose the following day's race.

This deed would certainly 'get the goat' of the horse's owner.

Bless you!

When somebody sneezes people often call out 'Bless you!' It is a custom which is thought to date back to the great plague in the seventeenth century when at least 80,000 people died in London alone.

A sneeze was believed to be the first sign of the horrific disease. But it's also said that in medieval times people believed that when a person sneezed his soul momentarily left his body.

So that the Devil could not capture the temporarily unguarded soul, by-standers quickly called 'God bless you!' The protected soul would then return to the safety of the body and the Devil would be thwarted.

Dressed to the nines

This saying simply means that you have put on your very smartest clothes, probably because you are off to an important function like a wedding, a formal dinner, or perhaps a job interview.

It is a very old expression and, although its origins are uncertain, it is believed to have started off as dressed 'to the eyes'. That meant, of course, smartly dressed from head to foot.

In medieval English the saying would have been 'dressed to then eyne'. Over the centuries it is thought to have gradually changed into 'to the nines'.

Waging a Battle Royal . . .

A keenly-fought contest between two people or two teams is said to be a 'Battle Royal'. It can refer to any game, from a chess tournament to a rugby match.

But it was no harmless pastime that gave birth to the saying – it was the horrific, now outlawed, 'sport' of cockfighting. Sixteen birds were pitted (put into a pit) against each other. The eight winners in the first 'round' were then matched and so on until just two cocks were left. The survivor was the 'king' – champion of the Battle Royal.

Soccer hooligans

Soccer hooligans have alas, figured all too often in the news in recent times.

The word hooliganism became established at the end of the nineteenth century when an Irish family named Hooligan lived in Southwark, south-east London. By all accounts they were such a rowdy, noisy and badly-behaved bunch that their reputation as trouble-makers spread far and wide.

Ever since, any group of youths who cause problems with their anti-social behaviour have been called 'hooligans'.

Face the music

If you are caught doing something wrong then (gulp!) you will just have to summon up all your courage and accept whatever punishment is coming. You will, in fact 'face the music'.

One theory says the saying comes from the plight of a nervous actor or entertainer who, when the curtain goes up, must literally face the music, as the orchestra is in the 'pit' in front of him.

Others think the expression dates back to the time when soldiers who were dismissed from the army for dishonourable conduct were drummed out of the service. They were literally 'facing the music'.

Ye olde tea shoppe

Places such as the famous Ye Olde Cheshire Cheese Inn in Fleet Street and Ye Olde Tea Shoppes throughout the country are said to be steeped in antiquity. So they may be. But their names are also steeped in error.

In the ancient alphabet used until the end of the middle ages the letters 'th' were represented by a single character which looked like our present 'y'. So when the word 'the' was transcribed from the old texts it was written down as 'ye'. It was never in fact pronounced as 'yee' and so to do so is nonsense. For what we have is the simple mis-spelling of the everyday word 'the'.

That has led to fanciful elaborations like Ye Olde Tea Shoppe. Ah well, don't tell ye touristes!

Bonfire night

We all know that bonfire night is held as a celebration on November 5 to mark the failure of Guy Fawkes and his fellow plotters to blow up the Houses of Parliament in 1605.

Bonfires go back a lot further than that. In the fifteenth century it had become a custom on a certain day to light three fires in honour of St John. Little is now known about the ceremony. But we do know that the first fire was made entirely of animal bones and was called a bone fire. The second, made only of wood, was a wood fire, and the third, wood and bones, was called St John's fire.

Our word bonfire comes of course, from the original, gruesome bone fire.

Worth his salt

Anybody 'worth his salt' is doing a good job, whether it's at work, as part of a team or in any situation where others rely on his efforts.

In Roman times, salt was considered vital for health and well-being, but often difficult to come by. So soldiers were actually paid partly in money and partly in salt. Later they were given an allowance so that they could buy their salt themselves and this money was known by the Latin name 'salarium' – meaning 'of salt'.

That's where our word salary – payment for work done – comes from.

What a load of old codswallop!

When somebody says something which is nonsense, far-fetched, or simply untrue, they are often accused of speaking 'a load of old codswallop'.

We have a certain American gent called Hiram Codd to thank for this colourful expression. In 1875 he patented a special bottle of mineral water which became very popular – except among hardened beer drinkers.

The word 'wallop' was already well in use to describe alcoholic drinks and so, sneeringly, Hiram's concoction – and other weak drinks – became known in bars as 'Codd's Wallop'. Gradually, anything inferior or false became known by the single word 'codswallop'.

Nest egg

Thrifty people who have regularly put away money in savings are often said to have built up 'a nice nest egg'. At one time, poultry farmers used to put a fake egg – usually made of porcelain – in a hen's nest, believing the bird would then be encouraged to lay more eggs. In the same way, a 'nest egg' came to refer to a person's savings.

The life of Reilly

Anybody living the 'life of Reilly' (sometimes spelt 'Riley') is surrounded by luxury and has no cares or worries.

The saying has emerged from the music hall days of the Victorian era. One popular song of the time was about an Irishman – actually named O'Reilly – who dreamed of the luxury life ahead once he made his fortune. The song was called 'Are you the O'Reilly?' and the chorus, which the audience sang, went: 'Are you the O'Reilly who keeps this hotel? Are you the O'Reilly they speak of so well? Are you the O'Reilly they speak of so highly? Cor blimey, O'Reilly, you are looking well'.

Black sheep of the family

In a large family there is bound to be a boy or girl who never seems to do well or is always in trouble. He or she is 'the black sheep of the family'.

For years, shepherds believed that black sheep were a problem: their coat was valueless and it was believed (wrongly) that their colour frightened other sheep. The expression gradually came to apply to troublesome humans.

The unkindest cut of all

These days we often hear of 'cuts' and when something cherished has to go – perhaps a hospital wing or a sports complex – the local newspaper might well refer to it as 'the unkindest cut of all'.

But the saying is no invention of a headline writer. It comes from Act III, scene two of Shakespeare's play, *Julius Caesar*. After the assassination of the emperor, Mark Anthony tells the Romans: 'This was the most unkindest cut of all.'

Shakespeare is the source of many popular sayings today. 'Mum's the Word' for example, comes from Henry IV, Part two; 'Seal your lips and give no words but – mum.'

Beating about the bush

Somebody who beats about the bush has the annoying habit of not saying exactly what they mean, but talking round the point.

It's a very old saying which comes from hunting. Specially hired people – known as 'beaters' literally beat bushes and startled game birds into the air. As soon as the waiting hunter saw his target in flight, he would immediately open fire. Unlike his colleague, he was a man of direct action and would certainly not be 'beating about the bush'.

That takes the cake

Originally this saying was used when somebody's efforts in a contest were so good that they were bound to carry off first prize. Later the expression was used mockingly of people who had said something silly or outrageous.

In the deep south of the United States in the last century negroes held competitions to see who could walk in the most graceful or imaginative way around a cake on the floor. The winner would literally 'take the cake'.

Merry Christmas

Wishing each other 'Merry Christmas' by sending a greetings card is a fairly new idea and one which had a troublesome beginning.

The first Christmas card to go on sale appeared in 1846. The picture on the front showed a family clearly in festive mood, happily drinking wine. And that's what caused the trouble. Church leaders and temperance organisations protested that the card depicted Christmas merely as a time for drinking and jollity. Nevertheless, sales went well.

In the 1870s a firm of art printers called Tucks began producing Christmas cards. The idea then really took off and developed into the multi-million pound business it is today.

Soap opera

Anybody who has never heard of J. R., Alexis Carrington or Bet Lynch and Pauline Fowler must have been living on a different planet lately. They are, of course, all characters from TV soap operas which attract millions of viewers every week.

The idea of serialised melodrama with a cliff-hanging finish to each episode is nothing new. They began in the United States when there were few television sets around and radio was at its popularity peak. At that time half a dozen or more serials were on the air each week. The link? They were nearly all sponsored by soap-makers. And so the phrase 'soap opera' was born.

New Scotland Yard

Scotland Yard is probably the most famous police headquarters in the world and the focus of countless films and books by thriller writers.

Detective work reveals that the centre got its name from the street where it was originally located, Great Scotland Yard, Whitehall. That name came from the site of a castle used 1,000 years ago by the kings of Scotland who had to travel down and stay there once a year to pay allegiance to the English court.

In 1967, New Scotland Yard was established in Broadway, Westminster.

The Jeep

The Jeep is, of course, the amazing four-wheel drive vehicle which is now popular all over the world.

It is so called because after it was designed in the US during the second world war it was listed by the army as a GP (general purpose) vehicle. The initials GP rapidly became the word 'Jeep'.

The army is also responsible for another well-used word in the motoring world, DERV – for use in a Diesel Engine Road Vehicle. You can now buy 'derv' from almost any garage.

Keep danger at bay

When people try to prevent the onset of a disaster, an illness, or some other unfortunate event, they are said to be 'keeping it at bay'. Over the centuries the bay laurel tree has been regarded by man as one of his great protectors. The Greeks and Romans, noting that the tree never seemed to be struck by lightning, used to wear its leaves on their heads as protection during thunderstorms.

Much later, during the Great Plague of London in 1665, people in their desperation turned to laurel leaves to protect them against the deadly affliction. They believed (wrongly – as 80,000 victims proved), that the leaves would keep the plague 'at bay'.

Between the devil and the deep blue sea

Somebody who is in a very difficult situation and is liable to be in real trouble whichever course of action he chooses is said to be 'between the devil the deep blue sea'. The devil in this case is not 'Old Nick', but the heavy wooden beam which used to be fixed to the sides of ships as a support for the big guns. It was called the gunwhale and was a very difficult place to get to, calling for great agility on the part of the luckless sailor ordered to that position.

One slip and . . . splash! He was literally between the devil and the deep blue sea.

A baron of beef

A baron of beef is a magnificent double slice of meat not separated at the backbone. A single slice is called a sirloin. It is said that Henry VIII was so enraptured by one mouth-watering hunk that he 'knighted' it – thus sir-loin. Nice story, but nonsense. The word is older than Henry VIII and comes from the French sur (over) and longe (loin).

But it is thought that some eighteenth-century English aristocrats named a double sirloin a 'baron' because a baron is a step up from a knight.

Staging a boycott

In the 1850s, a very strict and unbending retired English army officer, Captain Charles Cunningham Boycott, was a land agent on an estate in County Mayo, Ireland.

Because of several bad harvests, the tenants were very poor. But Boycott refused to reduce rents and ordered anybody in arrears to be evicted. His servants walked out and people refused to work for him.

In the end, he fled back to England – victim of the world's first 'boycott'.

A scapegoat

Somebody who is made to take the blame for the actions of another person is said to be a 'scapegoat'.

In the Old Testament, a goat is chosen to bear the sins of the people. It is led into the wilderness and abandoned, taking their sins with it.

Scape is believed to be a shortened form of escape. So in the Old Testament story the people 'escape' the responsibility of their sins by loading them on to the goat.

To get the sack

A person who has been dismissed from his job is often said to have 'got the sack'. Years ago this would have been true – literally. Because workmen used to own their own tools of trade and carry them round in a sack.

When they got a job the employer would look after their tools, but when the worker was no longer needed or wanted he would be given back his sack and told to look for work elsewhere.

Pop goes the weasel

Most of us remember the words of the nursery rhyme: 'Up and down the City Road; In and out the Eagle; That's the way the money goes; Pop goes the Weasel!'

Like most nursery rhymes, there is a story behind these seemingly meaningless words. The Eagle was the name of a pub in the City Road in London and it was a popular meeting place for people who worked in the hatmaking trade nearby. When short of funds some of them would 'pop' — that is, pawn — their weasel, or tool of their trade, to raise money for more drinks. Shame on them . . .

Wet behind the ears

Somebody who is not very experienced in life can make comments or express opinions that more mature people dismiss with a smile. They think the person has not shown a full understanding of the subject and say, 'Oh, he's still wet behind the ears'.

The expression is very old and refers to the fact that many animals, when they are born, have a small depression behind each ear. Of course, the creature is wet when new-born, and the last place to dry is the little area behind each ear. When that is dry, the animal is a little older and perhaps a little wiser.

He's a toady!

This saying is used to criticise somebody who, to further his own ends, says or does anything to please his superior.

It comes from the days of travelling medicine men in the American 'Wild West'. They used to sell usually useless potions to the public. Taking advantage of the popular but false belief that toads were extremely poisonous, the 'quack' doctor would get an accomplice to swallow, or pretend to swallow, a toad. He would then immediately drink one of the doctor's portions and, much to the amazement of the crowd, walk away fit and well.

A bear garden

If a father came into his sons' bedroom and found a pillow-fight in progress, he might shout: 'It's like a bear garden in here'. In effect, it is a place of turmoil and confusion.

In King Henry VIII's time, bear-baiting was very popular. So much so that gardens were set aside for the 'sport'. These 'bear gardens' were well known for scenes of utter chaos, shouting and fighting.

Scot-free

Scot, or sceot as it used to be spelt, was a form of taxation levied in olden times. Sometimes very poor people were excused payment. They were allowed to be sceot-free. Today the expression applies to anybody who gets out of a difficult situation unharmed.

The hair of the dog

After a party, it is not unusual for some of the guests to wake up the next morning with a hangover. The cure is said to be another drink, or 'the hair of the dog'.

This is based on the superstition that people who are ill after being bitten by a dog can only be cured by swallowing a piece of burnt hair from the same animal. In truth, the 'cure' seldom works.

Up the spout

When something is ruined, lost, broken or destroyed, it is 'up the spout'.

Pawnbrokers used to put goods brought into their shops into a lift which carried them to a storeroom. The lift was known as 'the spout'. Only when the customer could afford to pay back his loan – plus interest – were the goods brought back 'down the spout'.

America's Cup

This world-famous ocean-going yacht race got its name because of a bit of cheek on the part of the Americans.

The race began more than a hundred years ago and the idea was that the winning crew would be presented with a trophy – the Hundred-Guinea Cup – by the Royal Yacht Squadron.

Then the unthinkable happened. The United States entered a schooner, appropriately called *America* and won! The Yankee victors were so pleased with themselves that they promptly renamed the trophy America's Cup – and it's been that way ever since.

To bandy words

Bandying words means to quarrel with somebody. The phrase comes from the Irish game of bandy which is similar to hockey, though much older. The players bandy the ball from side to side with a stick that is crooked at the end, and try to force it into the opponents' goal.

The saying, 'I'll not bandy words with you', has come across the sea from Ireland.

Let the devil take the hindmost

Somebody who doesn't care too much about the result of his actions might well say: 'Let the devil take the hindmost'. It means that he is willing to take the risk and gamble that the result will be a success, for himself at least.

The saying is based on a medieval belief that the devil ran a training school for his followers. There was a leaving ceremony in which the 'students' had to run through a special underground passageway. The last person was 'the hindmost'. He was captured by the devil and had to stay as a slave.

Red herring

This is a saying often used in politics. It means a person is trying to confuse an argument by talking about something slightly, or even totally, different from the main point in dispute.

The expression is a very old one and comes from fox hunting. It was believed that red herrings – or bloaters – would destroy the scent of a fox if they were dragged across the animal's trail. The pursuing dogs would then be confused and probably follow a false trail. In fact they would be chasing a 'red herring'.

To come up to scratch

A person who passes a test or in some other way meets a required standard is said to have 'come up to scratch'.

The saying comes from the sport of prize-fighting, popular throughout Britain in the last century. There were no set rounds of three minutes, as is the case in boxing today. Instead the round went on until one of the fighters was knocked down.

Then, after a pause of 30 seconds, a count of eight began. If the fighter failed in that time to reach a mark scratched in the centre of the ring, he was beaten. He had failed 'to come up to scratch'.

The naked truth

If you tell the naked truth about somebody, it is the complete, absolute truth, including the bad points as well as the good ones.

The saying comes from an ancient fable in which Truth and Falsehood went for a swim in a lake. Falsehood got out first and put on Truth's clothes. But Truth could not bear the idea of dressing in Falsehood's garments, so he walked away naked.

THE NAKED TRUTH

Ship-shape and Bristol fashion

In the fifteenth century, Bristol was one of England's most important ports. Its biggest claim to sea-faring fame is that John Cabot and his three sons set off from Bristol in the reign of Henry VII to discover Newfoundland.

Survival on such perilous journeys in those days meant that the ships and equipment had to be in perfect working order. The men spent many hours making sure this was so. Anything that was well prepared, neat, tidy and efficient therefore came to be known as all 'ship-shape and Bristol fashion'.

Kick the bucket

Meat is delivered to market today in huge refrigerated lorries, ready to be sold and distributed to all parts of the country. But in years gone by, the animals were taken to the market on foot and the whole process was far more chaotic, messy and literally bloody.

The cattle, pigs and sheep were slaughtered after reaching the market and their sometimes still kicking bodies hung on a wooden frame which was known as a bucket beam. This gruesome piece of equipment gave rise to the expression, 'He's kicked the bucket', when referring to a person who had died.

His name is mud

John Wilkes Booth, the man who assassinated American President Abraham Lincoln in 1865, broke a leg while making his getaway. He called at the home of Doctor Samuel Mudd who treated his injury. The following day Dr Mudd was arrested and charged with conspiring to murder the President. He was sentenced to life imprisonment.

It was later established that Dr Mudd knew nothing of Booth's crime. He was pardoned and freed. But that could not prevent his name giving birth to the expression; 'His name is mud', referring to anybody who is thought of as disreputable or who is held in contempt.

Welsh Rabbit

This cheap and tasty snack is, of course, melted cheese on toast. It became known some 300 years ago and to start with was something of a joke. At that time only the rich could afford to pay for the game from the royal preserves in Wales, so ordinary people rarely had the chance of tasting rabbit. With dry humour they began referring to melted cheese on toast – one of the few dishes they could afford – as their 'Welsh Rabbit'.

In later years snobbish people – or perhaps menu writers – tried to make the dish sound more fancy by calling it 'Welsh Rarebit'.

Robbing Peter to pay Paul

People in financial difficulties sometimes try to juggle their money around in an attempt to solve their problems. They might pay one bill with money that should really have been used to pay somebody else. This is called 'robbing Peter to pay Paul'.

The expression goes back to the sixteenth century when urgent repairs were needed to St Paul's Cathedral but little cash was available for the purpose. To solve the problem the Abbey Church of St Peter, Westminster, which had been created a cathedral only ten years earlier in 1550, was 'demoted' back to an abbey church. Many of its estates – and the income from them – were appropriated to St Paul's. Thus, St Peter was 'robbed' to pay St Paul.

Talking gibberish

When somebody talks quickly and in a way that is difficult to understand they are said to be talking gibberish, which is pretty insulting to the man who gave birth to the saying: an eleventh century Arabian alchemist called Geber who was in fact very intelligent.

Because his scientific knowledge and discoveries would have been considered blasphemous and therefore very dangerous for Geber, he developed an obscure jargon so that he could write his work without fear of discovery. His notes were meaningless to anybody else: Just 'Geberish'.

Ringing the changes

If you are stuck in an uneventful job, or have to do the same task over and over again, you are likely out of sheer boredom to try to find different ways of going about it. That's known as 'ringing the changes'.

The saying comes, not surprisingly, from the art of bell-ringing. A set of three bells tuned to the diatonic scale can be rung in a series of six variations.

But somewhere with a set of twelve bells, such as Canterbury Cathedral, offers nearly 500 million variations. Somebody once calculated it would take thirty-eight years to ring all the changes at Canterbury!

A chip on his shoulder

Somebody who is by nature sulky, moody and argumentative, usually because he thinks others are against him, is said to have a chip on his shoulder.

Schoolboy rivals, particularly in America, gave birth to the saying nearly 200 years ago. It was the custom when two boys were spoiling for a fight for one to pick up a chip of wood and place it on his own shoulder. He would then challenge his opponent to knock it off. If the other boy did so, then they would begin to fight in earnest.

The V-sign

One of the most common gestures of anger today, often between car drivers, is the V-sign; two fingers raised upwards to the person who has annoyed you.

Its origins are uncertain, but one strong theory is that it began during the Hundred Years' War between England and France in the fourteenth and fifteenth centuries. Captured English archers had the two first fingers of their right hand cut off so that they couldn't take part in future battles.

It then became the custom of the English, after felling a Frenchman with an arrow, defiantly to raise his two fingers aloft to show he was still very much involved in the fight and as if to say; 'there's more where that came from!'

Sour grapes

When you have desperately tried to get something but failed at the last moment, you will want to hide your disappointment. The most common way to do that is to pretend that you were not really all that interested in the first place. That's known as 'sour grapes'.

The saying comes from Aesop's ancient Greek fable about a fox drooling over bunches of grapes in a vineyard. After exhausting himself by leaping up, over and over again trying to reach them, he eventually gives up and slinks away. The fox tries to cover his frustration by saying: 'They're as sour as crabs, anyway!'

In the nick of time

Something that happens 'in the nick of time' is a last moment reprieve from failure, like a goal at the end of extra time in a soccer match. And when the giant computerised scoreboard at a stadium like Wembley flashes up the message, 'Wow, what a goal!' it is only a modern version of a man with a stick of wood.

For hundreds of years the scores in games similar to soccer were kept by a man who would 'nick' the side of a tally stick each time a team scored. If victory came for one of the sides at the last moment, it was known as the 'nick in time'.

What a rigmarole

First you do this, then you do that, then you do another thing, then ... oh, 'what a rigmarole'! That's just what we call a long, involved, complicated way of doing things.

The 700-year-old expression began life as the Ragman Roll, given to King Edward I by Scottish noblemen. Each signed a deed pledging loyalty to the King and affixed his seal. The deeds were then joined together to form a document 40ft (12m) long!

The Ragman Roll is kept at the Public Records Office, London.